The Judicial Branch

By Tracy Vonder Brink

Table of Contents

A Starfish Book

Teaching Tips for Caregivers:

As a caregiver, you can help your child succeed in school by giving them a strong foundation in language and literacy skills and a desire to learn to read.

This book helps children grow by letting them practice reading skills.

Reading for pleasure and interest will help your child to develop reading skills and will give your child the opportunity to practice these skills in meaningful ways.

- Encourage your child to read on her own at home
- Encourage your child to practice reading aloud
- Encourage activities that require reading
- Establish a reading time
- Talk with your child
- Give your child writing materials

Teaching Tips for Teachers:

Research shows that one of the best ways for students to learn a new topic is to read about it.

Before Reading

- Read the "Words to Know" and discuss the meaning of each word.
- Read the back cover to see what the book is about.

During Reading

- When a student gets to a word that is unknown, ask them to look at the rest of the sentence to find clues to help with the meaning of the unknown word.
- Ask the student to write down any pages of the book that was confusing to them.

After Reading

- Discuss the main idea of the book.
- Ask students to give one detail that they learned in the book by showing a text dependent answer from the book.

The Judicial Branch

The U.S. government has three **branches**.

The judicial branch deals with laws.

Many **courts** make up this branch.

A court may have one or more **judges**.

A court may also have a **jury**.

A lawyer speaks for people in court.

The United States has laws.

Federal laws cover the whole country.

The judicial branch works with federal laws.

FEDERAL LAW

U.S. District Courts deal with rights.

They also judge people who have broken federal laws.

U.S. District Courts have a judge and a jury.

People who do not agree with the District Court may **appeal**.

Courts of Appeals may change a District Court's decision.

Or they may keep it.

Courts of Appeals have three judges and no jury.

UNITED STATES COURT OF APPEALS

People who do not agree with the Courts of Appeals may go to the Supreme Court.

The Supreme Court is the top court.

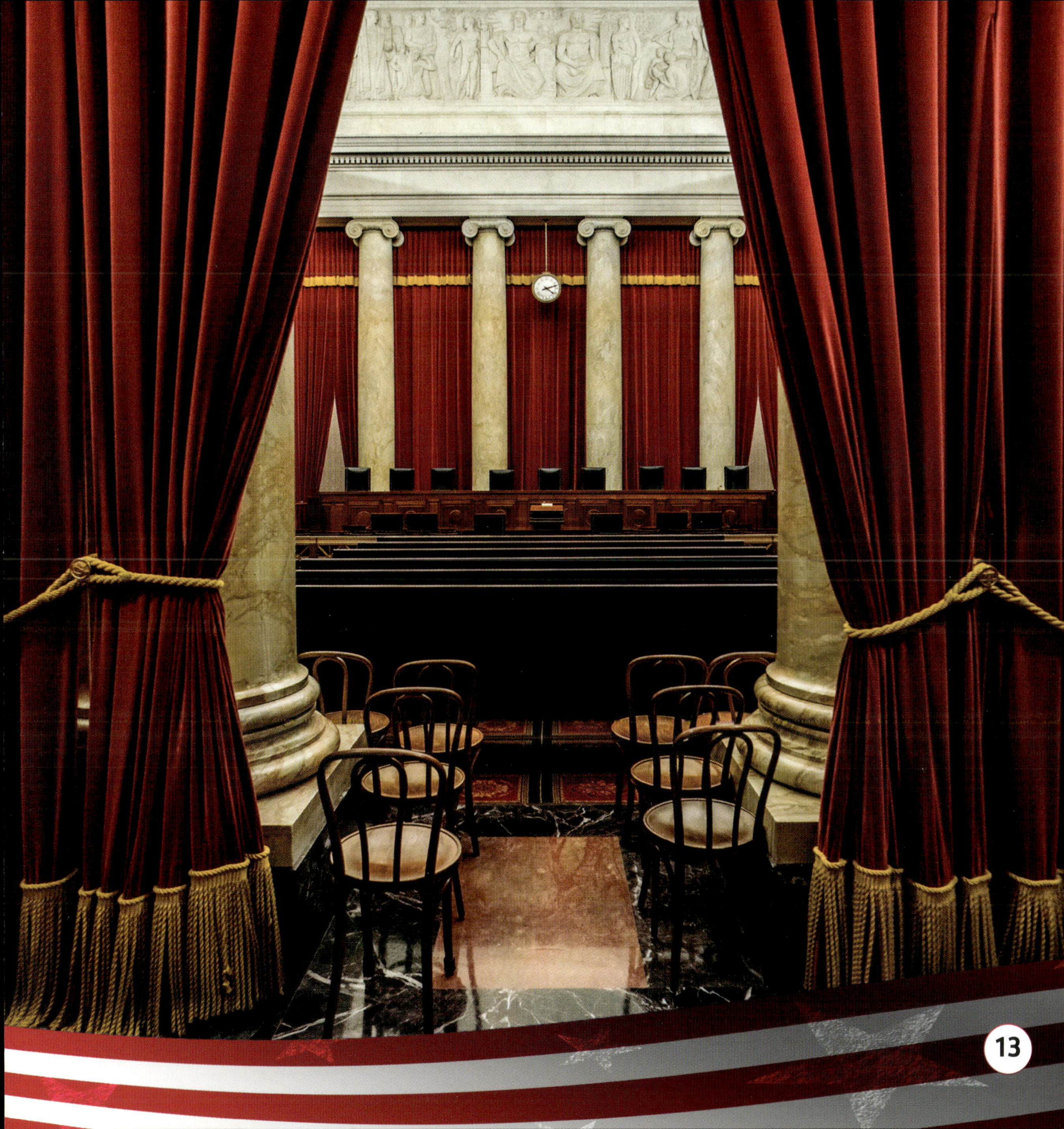

The U.S. Supreme Court has nine judges, called justices.

The president chooses them.

The **Senate** approves them.

The Supreme Court Justices in 2018.

The Supreme Court only hears the most important cases.

It may change the decision of any other court.

It may stop laws that do not agree with the Constitution.

We the People of the
insure domestic Tranquility, provide for the common
and our Posterity, do ordain and establish this
Article 1

The judicial branch decides if laws are fair.

It makes important decisions.

Words to Know

appeal (uh-PEEL): to ask to have a higher court accept or reject another court's decision

branches (BRANCH-ez): main parts of a government

courts (corts): places where law trials are held

federal (FEH-duh-ruhl): having to do with a central government

judges (JUHJ-ez): people with the power to make decisions on cases in a court of law

jury (JUR-ee): a group of people chosen to make a decision in a court of law

Senate (SEH-nut): one of two groups that makes up the U.S. Congress

Index

Comprehension Questions

1. How many branches of government are there?
   a. three b. four c. five
2. What does the word ***appeal*** mean?
   a. to ask the court to change their decision
   b. to ask for a new jury
   c. to ask for a new court date
3. Who listens to the most important cases?
   a. the District Courts
   b. the citizens
   c. the Supreme Court
4. **True or False:** The judicial branch decides if laws are fair.
5. **True or False:** The Supreme Court has 10 judges.

Answers
1. a 2. a 3. c 4. True 5. False

About the Author

Tracy Vonder Brink enjoys learning about the United States. She has visited the Supreme Court Building in Washington, D.C. Tracy lives in Cincinnati with her husband, two daughters, and two rescue dogs.

Written by: Tracy Vonder Brink
Design by: Kathy Walsh
Editor: Kim Thompson

Photographs/Shutterstock: Cover ©topseller, ©Lightspring, ©Tutti Frutti: Pg 1, 4-21 ©Lightspring, Pg 6, 8, 12, 14, 18 ©BCFC: Pg 3 ©Joe Ravi: Pg 4 ©sirtravelalot: Pg 5 ©sirtravelalot: Pg 7 ©create jobs 51: Pg 9 ©MR.Yanukit: Pg 11 ©Natalia Bratslavsky: Pg 13 ©stock_photo_world: Pg 15 ©Mandel Ngan: Pg 17 ©Aaron Smith / Smitty's Workshop: Pg 19 ©Victor Moussa: Pg 20 ©Joseph Sohm: Pg 21 ©@Wiki

Library of Congress PCN Data
The Judicial Branch / Tracy Vonder Brink
Civic Readiness
ISBN 978-1-63897-089-7 (hard cover)
ISBN 978-1-63897-175-7 (paperback)
ISBN 978-1-63897-261-7 (EPUB)
ISBN 978-1-63897-347-8 (eBook)
Library of Congress Control Number: 2021945258

Printed in the United States of America.

Seahorse Publishing Company
www.seahorsepub.com

Published in the United States
Seahorse Publishing
PO Box 771325
Coral Springs, FL 33077